Books are to be returned on or before
the last date below.

LIBREX-

The
Global
Marketplace

Booms, Bubbles, and Busts
The Economic Cycle

Barbara Gottfried Hollander

www.raintreepublishers.co.uk
Visit our website to find out more information about Raintree books.

To order:
☎ Phone 0845 6044371
📄 Fax +44 (0) 1865 312263
✉ Email myorders@raintreepublishers.co.uk

Customers from outside the UK please telephone +44 1865 312262

Raintree is an imprint of Capstone Global Library Limited, a company incorporated in England and Wales having its registered office at 7 Pilgrim Street, London, EC4V 6LB – Registered company number: 6695582

Edited by Adam Miller and Andrew Farrow
Designed by Ryan Frieson
Original illustrations © Capstone Global Library 2011
Illustrated by Planman Technologies (India) Pvt Ltd
Maps by Mapping Specialists Ltd
Picture research by Hannah Taylor
Originated by Capstone Global Library Ltd
Printed and bound in China by South China Printing Company Ltd

ISBN 978 0 431 00997 1 (hardback)
14 13 12 11 10
10 9 8 7 6 5 4 3 2 1

British Library Cataloguing in Publication Data
A full catalogue record for this book is available from the British Library.

Acknowledgements
We would like to thank the following for permission to reproduce photographs: Alamy Images pp. **12** (© Peter Casolino), **16** (© newstream rf), **19** (© Moon Yin Lam), **28** (© Bill Bachman); Corbis pp. **14** (Hulton-Deutsch Collection), **30** (Reuters/John C. Hillery), **40** (Richard T. Nowitz), **45** (epa/Andy Rain); Getty Images pp. **4** (Dove Shore), **7** (James Lauritz), **9** (Justin Sullivan), **20** (Hulton Archive), **23** (Bill Pugliano), **27** (Scott Olson), **32** (Alan Becker), **35** (Popperfoto/Rolls Press), **42** (Matt Cardy), **47** (Bill Pugliano); Photolibrary p. **36** (P Deliss).

Cover photograph of a screen showing a downturn in the stock market reproduced with permission of istockphoto (© Bjorn Meyer).

We would like to thank Michael Miller and Laura Hensley for their invaluable help in the preparation of this book.

Disclaimer
All the Internet addresses (URLs) given in this book were valid at the time of going to press. However, due to the dynamic nature of the Internet, some addresses may have changed, or sites may have changed or ceased to exist since publication. While the author and publisher regret any inconvenience this may cause readers, no responsibility for any such changes can be accepted by either the author or the publisher.

Contents

Some words are printed in bold, **like this**. You can find out what they mean by looking in the glossary.

The economic cycle

The year 2006 looked like a good one for business. Many of the world's leading **economies** had been growing at a steady pace for the past few years and showed no sign of slowing. People were working hard, and businesses were making money.

Adding fuel to the economic growth was the rapid rise in home **values**. People were becoming wealthier just by owning a home. It was easy to get a **loan** to buy a house. Homeowners could also easily borrow more money based on the increased value of their homes. They used that money to buy things, which kept businesses booming.

A new phase

A year later, the economic picture was looking dimmer. In the United States, the economy was growing more slowly. House prices were no longer rising, and more people were finding themselves unable to keep up with their mortgage payments.

By the middle of 2008, the economy was shrinking, not growing, and businesses were laying off workers. What was happening? In some ways the story is complicated. Yet people should not have been surprised that the good times ended. The economy was entering its next phase.

The economy

An economy is a system in which people make, sell, and buy **goods** and **services** (performed actions, such as car repairs). When you buy a new mobile phone or sell your old bike, you are part of the economy. Whenever people work, buy food, or pay **taxes** (payments to their government), they are also part of the economy.

Whenever you spend money on something such as a ticket for a gig, you put money into the economy.

Economies go through times of growth, called **expansions** or **booms**. This usually means there are more available jobs, more money earned for people to pay bills, and more shops open for business. An economy also goes through **downturns**, called **recessions** or **depressions**, during which the economy slows. This can mean job losses, less spending, and shops closing.

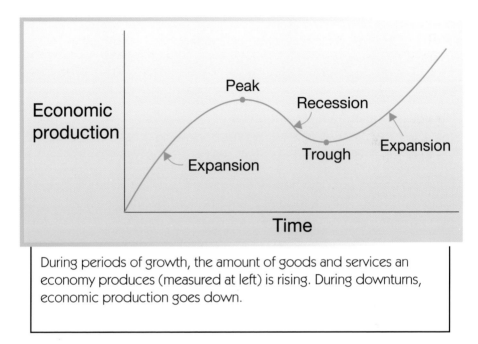

Peak
Recession
Economic production
Expansion
Trough
Expansion
Time

During periods of growth, the amount of goods and services an economy produces (measured at left) is rising. During downturns, economic production goes down.

Periods of economic growth and downturns form a **cycle**, or a repeating pattern. The beginning of an **economic cycle** is called a **peak**. This is the highest point of the growth phase. Then the economy begins to slow until it reaches its lowest point, known as the **trough**. Finally, the economy begins growing again until it reaches another peak.

Cycle lengths

Unlike many patterns, an economic cycle does not repeat itself at predictable times, such as once a year. Times of economic growth follow economic downturns, and economic downturns follow periods of growth. But the length of each expansion or **contraction** (shrinkage) is different for each cycle.

During periods of growth, more people may buy new homes and cars, take holidays, and save money for the future. During downturns, many people lose their jobs, their homes, and their savings. They may need to use their money to pay for food and housing, not new cars or holidays.

Economic indicators

The economic cycle is a repeating pattern of growths and downturns. But how can you tell which stage of the cycle the economy is in? **Economists** look at several ways to measure this. These measures are known as **economic indicators**.

As we will see, economic indicators tell economists important things about where an economy is in the economic cycle, such as:
- how much the economy is producing, or making
- how much money is being spent
- how much money is flowing between countries
- how many people are out of work
- how much money is available for borrowing and what it costs
- how much goods and services cost and how much money is worth.

These indicators not only help economists figure out where we are in the economic cycle. They also help them predict how long each phase of the cycle will last.

Gross Domestic Product

The main indicator that describes economic cycles is **Gross Domestic Product (GDP)**. GDP measures the total value of goods and services produced in a country in one year. **Consumption**, **investment**, government spending, and foreign trade are the four basic parts of GDP. When GDP is increases, the economy grows. This means that money is flowing through the economy. When GDP decreases, and the economy shrinks, less money is flowing through the economy because spending has slowed down.

Consumption

Personal, or private, consumption (buying things) is the biggest part of GDP in most countries. It tells economists part of the story of how much money is being spent. In **industrialized** countries, such as the United States, United Kingdom, Canada, and Australia, consumption is about 60 percent of total output. When people (called **consumers**) buy goods, such as new clothes, electronics, and cars, they are consuming. Buying services, like seeing a film or getting a haircut, is also part of consumption. Consuming goods and services makes money flow into the economy.

Investment

Investments are another part of GDP. Investments are when people buy financial products, with the hope of making more money. Investments that affect GDP include when people put money into building new factories, when people buy machines, when they pay for goods in warehouses that will be sold on shop shelves, and when they build new houses.

People make investments to start companies or to help existing ones grow. Investments are important because they lay the foundation for future production. By making investments, people help fuel the economy.

Government spending

Another part of GDP is the money governments spend. Governments pay for things such as new roads, rubbish collection, and schools. They also provide money for things like medical research, space exploration, and military equipment. Since GDP measures production, the only government spending included is money spent on goods and services. Money given by the government to the people, such as scholarships, is not included in GDP.

Imports and exports

Another aspect of GDP is how money goes between countries via **imports** and **exports**. When you buy a computer that is made in Japan, you are purchasing an import, or an item from a foreign country. And the Japanese are exporting (sending out) the computer to your country.

GDP takes into account both imports and exports. To arrive at the official GDP figure, economists add in the money from exports (money that flows into the country) and subtract the money from imports (money that flows out of the country). If the value of the imports is greater than the value of the exports, the country has a **trade deficit**. If the exports are worth more than the imports, the country has a **trade surplus**. Countries such as the United States and United Kingdom have trade deficits, while China has a trade surplus.

Busy container ports like this one in Melbourne, Australia, are places where exported and imported goods travel on their way to the marketplace.

The job market

Another important economic indicator is how many people are out of work. Whatever the state of the economy, some people will always be out of work. This can happen because individual businesses are not doing as well as their competitors and cannot hire new people. Other times, people are out of work because the economy, or GDP, is shrinking.

Unemployment

Countries have government agencies that track national **unemployment rates**. The unemployment rate is the percentage of working-age people who do not have jobs and are actively looking for new jobs.

Frictional unemployment

Frictional unemployment happens when people leave their job to look for another one, or when students finish school and start looking for work. During this time, people may take a break from work or look for other careers.

Unemployment benefits

Unemployment benefits are payments and other benefits that governments give to people without jobs. When people are working, they are making payments to the government. When they lose their jobs through no fault of their own, they are entitled to money and other benefits while they seek new jobs.

Unemployed people who receive benefits must meet certain requirements. For example, a person must be actively looking for another job. How people lose their jobs can also affect whether or not they receive these benefits. A person who quit a job may not be entitled to certain benefits.

In the United Kingdom, unemployed people who are looking for work receive jobseeker's allowance. Depending on their age and circumstances they might also be eligible for other benefits, such as help with housing costs or council tax.

Some people who receive benefits fall into the "unemployment trap". Because they are receiving money, some people do not feel the need to find a new job. But unemployment benefits are often much less than the money that can be earned from working.

People who lose their jobs often get retrained to learn new skills. They are then qualified to apply for more jobs.

Structural unemployment

Structural unemployment is caused when something creates a mismatch between skills and jobs. For example, in the United States and Europe, many textile jobs have been outsourced or sent to factories in Asia. These skilled textile makers have lost their jobs due to structural unemployment.

Cyclical unemployment

Cyclical unemployment happens when people lose their jobs because the economy is growing more slowly, or contracting. During an economic downturn, businesses are not making as many goods and services. So, they do not need as many workers. Some companies may even close.

For example, in December 2007 at the beginning of the economic downturn, only 813,000 people were out of work in the United Kingdom. This is about the same number of people that live in the city of Leeds. By February 2010, well into the economic downturn, the number of people unemployed had risen massively to 2.5 million.

Seasonal unemployment

Did you ever notice that shopping centres are busier in December than in other months? That is because people are shopping for Christmas gifts. Businesses hire extra workers to help the additional customers. But once the festive season is over, these extra workers lose their jobs.

This is known as seasonal unemployment. This type of unemployment happens because there are certain times of the year that more workers are needed, and other times that require fewer workers. There are other examples of seasonal unemployment, too. Ski lodges typically need more workers during the winter months. But construction workers usually have more work during the warmer months.

The flow of money

The flow of money is another important economic indicator. The amount of money available in an economy is controlled by a **central bank**. Most countries have central banks, and a large part of their job is to try to affect and respond to the economic cycle.

Money supply

A central bank has a few tools that it uses to speed up economic growth or slow it down. These tools change the amount of money in the system, also known as the money supply.

A central bank can increase or decrease the amount of money in the economy. This can influence the price of borrowing money, called the **interest rate**. Increasing the amount of money in the economy usually causes interest rates to drop. When the growth of the money supply slows, interest rates go up. An interest rate is the amount of money paid or received over the course of a year, as a percentage of the amount borrowed or loaned.

WHAT IT MEANS TO ME   ### How interest works

How does **interest** work, exactly? When you take out a loan from the bank, you are charged interest on the loan. Interest is the additional money owed in exchange for borrowing money from someone. You will have to pay back the original amount of the loan (called the principal) plus the interest on your loan. The interest payments depend on the principal and on the interest rate. For example, if you took out a £100 loan and the bank charges a 10 percent **annual** interest rate, then you would owe £10 in interest at the end of one year – in addition to eventually paying back the principal.

Earning interest

For a borrower, interest is an extra price to pay for taking out a loan. But for a lender, such as a bank, interest is the money earned for loaning out money.

When a borrower pays interest to a bank, the bank earns this money. So, the bank makes an investment by giving out the money in the first place, and then it earns the extra interest payments in return for this investment. This is one way banks stay in business. How much the bank earns partly depends on the interest rate. Banks take in a lot of money from interest – and they can give this money out as loans, which keeps the economic cycle moving.

Interest rates and the economic cycle

How do rising or falling interest rates affect the economic cycle? Interest rates are important because they affect how expensive it is to borrow money.

If interest rates drop, then borrowing becomes less expensive, and more people and businesses will receive loans and spend the money they receive. When people and businesses spend, money flows into and through the economy, helping it to grow.

But when interest rates rise, borrowing money becomes more expensive. Fewer people and businesses borrow money, and less money flows into and through the economy. This causes economic growth to slow.

Interest rates have a huge effect on economic indicators like production and spending. This in turn has a big effect on where in the economic cycle an economy is.

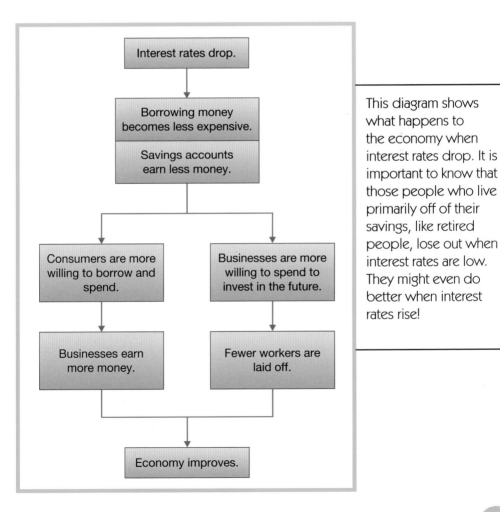

Interest rates drop.

Borrowing money becomes less expensive.

Savings accounts earn less money.

Consumers are more willing to borrow and spend.

Businesses are more willing to spend to invest in the future.

Businesses earn more money.

Fewer workers are laid off.

Economy improves.

This diagram shows what happens to the economy when interest rates drop. It is important to know that those people who live primarily off of their savings, like retired people, lose out when interest rates are low. They might even do better when interest rates rise!

Prices

As we have seen, a central bank influences interest rates by changing the amount of money in the economy. But increasing and decreasing the money supply does more than that. It also affects the value of your money.

Changes in prices (see box below) are another important economic indicator that economists use to study the economic cycle.

Supply, demand, and price

The price of something can change for many reasons, including in reaction to the laws of **supply** and **demand**.

When a business charges a higher price for a good or service, it earns more money from each sale. It can use this extra money to make more products. If the business sells more products, it earns even more money. So, higher prices mean that a company is willing to supply products. This is known as the "law of supply".

Supply is only half the economic story. Demand is just as important. Suppliers can always offer their goods and services, but consumers must be willing and able to buy them. This is where price comes in. Price can cause people to demand products – or to not want them at all. What happens to the amount demanded as price increases? It goes down, because as things become more expensive, people buy less (or not at all). That is the "law of demand".

Changes in prices for everyday goods, such as supermarket food, can affect their sales. If items are priced cheaply, consumers might choose to buy more of them.

Deflation

When there is not enough money in the economy, the price of commonly used goods and services (such as food, a haircut, and petrol) decreases. This is called **deflation**. Because goods are becoming less expensive, deflation makes people want to hold onto their money. After all, an item that you want will only cost less tomorrow. This can cause economic growth to slow.

Inflation

When a central bank puts more money into the economy, goods and services become more expensive. A rise in the general price level of goods and services over time is called **inflation**. Inflation has the opposite effect on spending as deflation. Since the prices of goods and services are rising, people are more likely to buy products today. After all, things will only cost more tomorrow. So, inflation puts more money into the economy. This can lead to an upturn in the economic cycle.

But sometimes a central bank puts in too much money and creates too much of a demand for products. Then, the result is even higher inflation. And if your **income** (money earned) does not rise, too, then inflation takes away some of your purchasing power, or the value of what you can buy. Your money can no longer buy what it used to, because it is losing its value. This can have a negative effect on the economy.

Different kinds of inflation

There are different kinds of inflation. Monetary inflation is when the general price level rises because there is more money in the economy. Price inflation comes from other factors, such as a rise in costs for businesses.

Rising costs

Businesses have costs associated with the products that they make. If something becomes more expensive to make, then it usually becomes more expensive to buy. In other words, the extra costs are passed along as a higher price to the buyer. This is called cost-push inflation.

One business cost is **wages**, or money paid to workers. If a business needs to pay more money to its workers, it may raise prices in order to not lose money. This type of inflation is called wage-push inflation. Like all kinds of inflation, it is an indicator that affects the economic cycle.

Inflation and fixed incomes

If people's wages rise as the price of goods and services increases, then they will still be able to afford products. But what about people whose wages do not rise with inflation, or people on "fixed incomes", such as retired people who live off savings and the interest they earn from investments? If interest rates do not rise but prices do, these people can no longer afford their way of living. When inflation strikes, these groups are the most affected.

Hyperinflation

Hyperinflation occurs when inflation rises at an extreme pace. When this happens, a country's **currency** (money) becomes essentially worthless. Prices are rising every day, so people rush out to buy things before their money loses more value. Hyperinflation occurred in Germany in the 1920s, as the country struggled to pay its **debts** from World War I (1914–18). The value of a German mark went from 60 marks per US dollar in early 1921 to 4.2 trillion marks per dollar in late 1923! Some workers were paid three times a day, so they could spend the money before prices went up! Millions of people saw their savings lose their value. Eventually, the German mark was replaced by a new currency.

Hyperinflation occurred more recently in Zimbabwe. At its peak in 2008, prices were doubling almost every day. The country began issuing currency with larger and larger values, such as the 100 trillion dollar bill. Eventually, people stopped using the Zimbabwe dollar and switched to other currencies, such as the US dollar.

After World War I, the German mark lost so much value that it was almost worthless. Here, German children in the 1920s play with money on the street.

Know your indicators

This table will help you review the different economic indicators you have read about in this chapter. You can use your knowledge of economic indicators to guide you in changing your spending habits, figuring out a good job direction, and even calculating how much a car **loan** will cost. The next time you read a newspaper, remember that:

ECONOMIC INDICATOR		
Gross Domestic Product (GDP) expansion or contraction	affects	your selection of goods and services.
Personal consumption	is about	how much money people spend on goods and services.
Business investment	says a lot about	whether or not a company is growing – and if it might be hiring more workers in the future.
Exports	are about	selling goods and services to other countries, which increases the GDP and helps the economy.
Imports	are about	buying goods from other countries, like foreign-made cars and computers, which lowers the GDP.
Unemployment rate	tells you	how easy it might be to get a new job.
Money supply	affects	the amount of money available for individuals and businesses to borrow.
Interest rates	tell you	about the cost of borrowing money.
Changes in prices often	tell you	whether the economy is experiencing deflation or inflation.

Economic booms

Economic indicators tell you where the economy is in its cycle, including periods of expansion, or growth. Many things can spur economic booms – and the biggest is spending!

People like economic booms. It means more jobs, more money to spend, and more goods and services to buy. Businesses like economic booms, too, because they increase production, earn more money, and grow.

Let's spend

Economic growth is usually measured by increases in GDP, and most of the GDP is personal consumption. When people spend money, the economy grows. During an expansion, people buy more goods and services than they do when the economy is not growing. People also tend to borrow more money through loans and **credit** cards. Then, they use this borrowed money to buy even more goods and services.

Economic booms encourage people to invest in their futures, including buying new homes.

More consumption, more investment

When people are buying more goods and services, businesses make more products to sell to them. To increase production, companies may build more factories and open more stores. The money that companies spend on expanding their businesses and producing more goods and services (their investment) also keeps the economy growing.

When businesses are selling more products, they need to hire more workers to keep up their supply. When new employees are hired, the unemployment rate can go down. These new workers also use their **salaries**, or money earned from working, to buy goods and services.

More consumption, more profits

When companies sell more goods, they take in more money. More sales can also mean more **profits**. A company has **expenses**, or money that it spends to run the business. It also has income, called **revenue**, that is received when goods and services are sold. Revenue minus expenses equals profit.

Companies can use their profits to **invest** in (put money into) their businesses and help them grow even more. Companies can also give some of the profit to their shareholders, who own the businesses (see page 19). This payment is known as a **dividend**. Both investments and people's use of the dividend money can help the economy grow.

Spending by borrowing

Both people and businesses often borrow money to pay for their expenses. As we have seen (see pages 10 and 11), interest rates are the cost of borrowing money. Low interest rates encourage both businesses and people to borrow money. This is because they make borrowing less expensive. So, when central banks lower interest rates, they can increase investments and personal consumption, which fuels an economic expansion.

Borrowing in the boom

After the 2000 to 2007 economic boom, many people in the UK and USA were worse off than before the cycle began. While incomes in many households went up during the boom, they did not go up as fast as the cost of living. (Cost of living includes common and necessary goods and services, such as food, mortgage payments, council tax, and petrol.) So, in the end they were not able to buy as much as they could at the start of the boom.

How did these people try to keep their standard of living steady? They borrowed. Millions took out loans and ran up large credit card bills. They also borrowed money based on the increasing value of their homes. They hoped they could then pay back the money over time – but many could not.

Government's role

Increases in government spending also fuel economic growth temporarily. Governments can directly spend money on goods and services, such as paying construction workers to build new roads. Governments can also lower taxes to help the economy. When a government lowers the amount people have to pay in taxes, it gives people more money to spend. This extra spending adds to economic growth. (For more on taxes, see page 28.)

Increase in confidence

People consume, or buy, more goods and services when they believe that the economy will continue to grow. This is called **consumer confidence**.

For example, if people believe that they will have their jobs in the future, then they will be more likely to spend money. They do not have to think as much about saving money. In contrast, if people think that they might lose their jobs in a month, then they will spend less money. They want to save money in case they lose their jobs. Therefore, an increase in consumer confidence fuels economic growth.

The same idea applies to businesses. Believing that the economy will grow in the future will make businesses more likely to make investments. After all, a growing economy means more demand for products. And businesses want to sell more products to make more money. So, if a business believes that it will be able to sell more products in the future, it will invest in its growth today, such as building factories.

Higher standards of living

During economic booms, people usually enjoy a higher **standard of living**. The standard of living is the level of comfort that you feel from having goods, services, and luxury items available to you. Economists often measure a country's standard of living by the **GDP per capita**. This is a country's GDP divided by the number of people living in the country.

When the economy is growing, total output is rising and more goods and services are available to consumers. Wages can also increase. Then, people have even more money to spend on a bigger selection of goods and services.

However, GDP per capita does not measure how much of the wealth is shared by the people in these countries, or how many people live in poverty. Even when GDP per capita is rising, many people can be left out if most of the increased wealth goes to a small group of people.

Increased risk

Economic booms give people and businesses more confidence in the economy. But sometimes this confidence leads people and businesses to take on too much **risk**. Risk is making a decision knowing that the result could turn out differently than expected. During recent economic booms, both people and businesses borrowed a lot of money, because they believed that a growing economy would allow them to pay it back. Unfortunately, economic booms do not last forever, and people are often unable to pay back what they have borrowed.

Shares and the wealth effect

During periods of economic growth, people often benefit from a rise in the **stock market**. This is the place where people buy and sell investments like shares (also called stocks) in companies. Many people, and organizations such as banks and retirement funds, invest in shares as a way of earning more money.

When companies are making a profit, or when investors believe the fortunes of a business will improve, more people buy shares in the company. This causes its share prices to rise. This higher price earns money for those who bought the shares at a lower price. For example, if a person buys 500 shares at £10 per share and sells them at £15 per share, then the shareholder makes £2,500 when he or she sells the shares.

When share prices rise, people feel wealthier, because they have an investment with a value that is going up. (They do not actually see this money, however, unless they sell the shares.) People may be more willing to spend money as a result of this potential wealth. This is known as the "wealth effect."

There is an idea in economics known as the "wealth effect". It says that as people become (or even feel) wealthier, they spend more money.

Historical booms

Throughout history, people have enjoyed economic booms during which their standards of living increased. Companies have also enjoyed higher profits and growth during these booms, as people bought more of their products.

Growth in Asia

In 2002 the Japanese economy pulled out of a decade-long slump (see page 33) and grew for 69 months – its longest boom since World War II (1939–45). The Chinese economy also grew during this time. In fact, while it took 50 years for both the United Kingdom and United States to double their GDP per capita (their standard of living), China did it in around 10 years! As we have seen, GDP per capita is GDP divided by the number of people. This is even more impressive when you consider that China has more than 1.3 billion people.

There are many reasons for the growths of these Asian economies, including investments such as expanding businesses. More people in the labour force (especially women) and the movement of workers from farms to businesses in the cities have helped boost growth. Asian countries also export a lot of goods and services. In fact, Asia accounts for 30 percent of **global** (worldwide) trade, and China is one of the top-three trading countries in the world.

United States

One famous economic expansion in the United States came in the 1920s. This period was known as the "roaring twenties" because of the fun, fast-paced lifestyle that some people enjoyed as their standard of living rose. The economic expansion was fuelled by low interest rates and easy-to-get credit, which encouraged consumers to spend. This period ended when the stock market crashed in 1929 (see page 34).

Although the "roaring twenties" was great for some, many Americans did not see their standard of living improve during this time.

The longest economic expansion in the United States began in 1991 and ended in 2001. More recently, an expansion in the United States began in 2002 and ended in late 2007. Low interest rates and easy credit helped the economy grow more quickly, just as it did in the 1920s. And like the 1920s, the end of this era included a crash in stock prices, this time in 2008.

The United Kingdom's longest economic boom

In 1992 the United Kingdom began its longest economic boom. Its economy grew for 16 years. People were spending money on goods and services. Businesses were making money, growing, and hiring new workers. By December 1999, Britain's unemployment rate was the lowest it had been in 20 years – and, for the first time, it was lower than the US rate. Exports were growing, as the United Kingdom was selling more goods to other countries. Share prices increased as companies made more money and people wanted to buy their shares. But, as we will see, this boom would not last.

Economic booms around the world

The last part of the 1990s and the early 2000s was a time of economic growth around the world. People borrowed and spent more money, and they often enjoyed a higher standard of living. Companies made more money and expanded. Share prices rose and unemployment fell.

Many countries' total output, or GDP, was growing even more than their **trend growth rates**. A trend growth rate is an average growth rate for an economy in the long run. At this rate, the economy is growing at a safe and good speed. When the economy is growing faster than this rate, it is in an economic boom.

For example, the United Kingdom's trend growth rate tends to be about 2.5 percent annually. But during the boom, its GDP was growing at 3.5 percent and 4.0 percent annually. Most trend growth rates of industrialized nations are between 2 and 2.5 percent annually. But some countries have different rates. China's trend rate is even higher, at around 8 to 9 percent. So, when China's economy is growing at 10 percent, China is in an economic boom.

But all good things must come to an end, including booms, as we will see in the next chapter.

Economic downturns

As part of the economic cycle, booms hit their highest points (called peaks). Then the economy begins a downturn – a period full of less consumption, job losses, and business failures.

The downturn begins – and continues

As a downturn begins, consumers slow their spending for many reasons, including job losses or less confidence in the economy (see page 18). People also need to spend less if they borrow less money. Higher interest rates (the cost of borrowing money) or less available credit can reduce borrowing.

And when consumers slow their spending, there is a domino effect. If you line up a row of dominoes and then push the first domino, what happens? The first domino falls onto the domino behind it, and this continues until all the dominoes fall down.

In the case of the economy, less spending means that companies do not sell as many goods and services. Then, businesses do not have as much money to make new investments, such as expanding their production. If people continue to cut back on their spending, businesses are often forced to cut prices to sell their products. Some businesses may even close. Both reduced production and closings mean that people lose their jobs. And when people are not earning money, they cannot buy as much. This further reduces spending, and the cycle continues, making the economic downturn even worse.

International connections

Money travels worldwide: companies open businesses in foreign countries, governments invest in other countries, people invest in foreign companies, and countries both import and export goods and services. There are many business advantages to the global connection, including selling to bigger markets and having more ways to produce goods, such as workers.

But there are also disadvantages. Remember the domino effect? This happened in the last US recession, which ended up being part of a global recession. When US companies with foreign offices failed, the offices in the foreign countries closed, too. This meant that both the workers in the United States and in the foreign countries lost their jobs. It also meant that people who invested in these companies lost their money.

And when Americans slowed their spending, they not only bought fewer US goods, they also bought fewer foreign-made goods. For example, Americans buy a lot of foreign cars, especially Toyotas and Hondas from Japan. But during the recession, Americans slowed their spending. In November 2008, Toyota recorded its lowest rate in decades. The following month, Toyota reported its first loss in operating profit in 70 years.

WHAT IT MEANS TO ME — Companies and downturns

Bankruptcy happens when a business cannot repay its debts (the money it owes). During economic downturns, both individuals and businesses have more trouble paying their expenses, including repaying borrowed money. Here are some shops that have disappeared from the British High Street:

- Woolworths   • Virgin Music   • MFI

- Borders Bookshops   • MK One   • Rosebys

Here are some US companies that have closed many shops during the economic downturn:

- Ann Taylor (clothing)

- Foot Locker (shoes)

- KB Toys

- Pier 1 (housewares)

- Sprint Nextel (telephone services)

- Starbucks

- Zales (jewellery).

The bankruptcy of General Motors, based in Detroit, USA, had repercussions around the world.

What is a recession?

Economic downturns happen when people spend less. People demand fewer goods and services. As we have seen (see page 12), demand is about the amount of goods that people are willing and able to buy. When people demand fewer products, then eventually companies supply fewer products. This leads to a fall in economic activity.

Falling GDP

A recession is a sustained fall in economic activity. It is an economic downturn in which the GDP falls. As we have seen, most economists measure economic activity by GDP (see pages 6–7). There can be many different reasons for this decline.

During a recession, the biggest drop in the GDP almost always comes from a fall in consumption of **durable goods** – goods that last three years or more, such as cars. When people stop spending money, a country's economy slows down. During the worldwide recession that began in 2008, people stopped spending money. As people continued not to spend, the recession became even worse.

WHAT IT MEANS TO ME | **Experiencing a recession**

Imagine that you had a part-time job mowing lawns. In an economic boom, people in your neighbourhood have money to spend, so they hire you to mow their lawns. You make £100 a month. You save some of your money, but spend £20 a month on snacks at your corner shop. The shop makes a profit from your purchases.

Then a recession hits. Some of the people whose lawns you mow are out of work. They mow their own lawns now. Others are afraid of losing their jobs, so they save money by waiting longer between mowings. Now you only make £70 a month. With less money to spend, you stop buying snacks at the corner shop. Since you do not know when things will get better, you save all of your money.

As a result of the recession, you have just decreased the GDP. It went down by £30 when your lawn mowing business slowed down, and another £20 when you stopped buying snacks from the shop. This example also shows how tough times can be contagious. That shopkeeper is now earning less money from you and may reduce his spending to make up for changes to his business like this. The effects will be felt throughout the economy.

A decrease in other parts of the GDP can also reduce output. When businesses stop making investments or countries decrease exports or increase imports, the GDP decreases (see box below). Less government spending also reduces the GDP.

Figure it out

Economists record the GDP over a three-month period called a quarter. Then, they study the difference in GDP from one quarter to the next to see if the economy is growing or shrinking. Many economists feel that a recession occurs when the total output of a country, or the "real" (adjusted for inflation) GDP, falls for about two quarters (or six months). Other economists define a recession by looking at other economic indicators, too, such as the level of employment.

Fear and gloom

When a recession hits, it is all over the news, as newspapers, magazines, and websites report economic growth (or lack thereof), unemployment figures, and other statistics. People and businesses respond with fear and gloom. Recessions are felt across the economy – and the world.

Falling exports

From 2003 to 2007, China's economy grew by at least 10 percent each year. In 2008 China's economy grew 9 percent. But from January to March 2009, China's GDP slowed to 6.1 percent growth. What happened? China's exports fell by 17 percent in March 2009.

This decrease in exports led to businesses selling fewer goods and services. As businesses sold less, their profits went down, too. Eventually, businesses had to cut costs. Workers lost their jobs, and unemployment in China went up.

The job market

As we have seen, during a recession people lose their jobs, and so the unemployment rate rises. The loss of their salary can make it difficult for people to pay their bills. They may cut back on buying goods or services they want but do not need, such as new cars or entertainment.

A recession also means that many companies are decreasing their production or are closing altogether, which makes it harder for people to find a new job. With more people out of work, the demand for products made by businesses also decreases. This can lead businesses to cut costs even more, including sacking more workers. These people are now out of work, too – and competing for the few jobs that are available with people who were already out of work. Less demand and job losses can form another cycle, making the economic downturn last even longer.

WHAT IT MEANS TO ME   **Dealing with job loss**

When the recent recession began in the United States, international car manufacturers Chrysler and General Motors, based in the state of Michigan, were hit hard. Their sales fell, and soon these car makers were unable to pay their bills.

All of this affected the people who worked for these companies. In August 2000 about 200,000 people in Michigan did not have jobs. By August 2009 this number more than tripled to almost 700,000. Most of these workers have families. Some people decided to leave Michigan in search of work.

How would you feel if one of your parents lost his or her job? How do you think your family's spending habits would be affected? What if you had to move away from your home, your school, and your friends? Dealing with unemployment can be difficult, forcing all members of a family to cut back on the things they want and to make other sacrifices.

The stock market

During an economic downturn, share prices drop. Like goods and services, share prices are determined by supply and demand (see page 12). When people have less money to invest and less confidence in the future of companies, there is less demand for share investments. This causes the prices of shares to drop.

Shares can be risky investments. During a recession, many companies earn less money, and some go out of business. This means that there is also less of a chance that investors will make money. The uncertain prospects of many companies can cause share prices to fall further.

Sometimes a recession can be preceded by a rapid crash in share prices. The most famous of these occurred in October 1929, when share prices in the United States dropped 25 percent over two days, and continued to fall as the United States and other countries fell into the Great Depression (see page 34).

More recently, in October 2008, the stock market dropped 22 percent over eight days as the world began dealing with a financial crisis. By that time, the world had been in a recession for several months, but the worst was yet to come.

People who work in the stock market experience the drama of rapid rises and drops in share prices.

The credit market

The **credit market** is made up of people who borrow and lend money. Lenders make loans, or offer credit, and expect to be paid back. When borrowers cannot repay their loans, lenders have less money to lend. This makes for a tight credit market, which further reduces spending and worsens economic downturns. (See pages 36 to 39 for more on credit.)

Dealing with a recession

Both a country's government and its central bank work to shorten recessions and reduce their harmful effects. They share the same goals – to get people to spend money and get companies to hire more people!

Cutting taxes

As we have seen, governments can encourage people to spend money by putting more money into the hands of the people. One way they can do this is by lowering taxes, the money that people pay governments for basic services. Then, people can use this extra money to buy things.

In 2009, governments around the world cut taxes to encourage economic growth. For example, the US government tried to spur economic growth by putting more money into the hands of consumers. It gave out tax rebates that added US$80 billion to the US debt, but only increased consumption by about US$20 billion. Most people saved the rest of the money or used it to pay off bills. So, these tax rebates did not lead to a significant increase in economic activity. The UK government cut the Value Added Tax (VAT) temporarily by 2.5 percent. The VAT is a form of tax on goods and services that are used for consumption.

KINDS OF TAXES	
Income tax	Tax on money earned
Council tax	Tax on the value of your house or other property
Sales tax	Tax on products sold to consumers
Value added tax	Tax on goods and services used to make and sell consumer products
Inheritance tax	Tax on money and goods inherited after a death

During a recession, many governments try to get as much money flowing into the economy as possible. One of the methods used by the UK government in 2008-2009, was **quantitative easing**.

Increasing spending

Another way governments can help during a recession is through spending. The government can extend unemployment insurance and other programmes that help people who are out of work. They can also start projects that put people to work, such as building roads and bridges. These measures put money into the hands of workers, who can then spend it to help boost the economy. (This spending money comes in part through the sale of government **bonds**, which individuals and other governments purchase as a safe form of investment.)

Many governments spent large sums to help their economies in 2009. China spent 4 trillion yuan (US$586 billion), while Spain spent more than 8 percent of its GDP on public works programmes alone. Debt is a real problem for many countries. In 1988 the total US debt was equal to half of the GDP. But by 2009 it was 85 percent of the GDP. This means the US government owed almost as much as the economy produced in 2009. In contrast, UK debt was about 55 percent of its GDP.

The paradox of thrift

Saving your money is a good idea. But if everyone saves during a recession, it can cause a problem.

The main way to lift an economy out of a recession is to increase personal spending. This happens when people buy more goods and services. So, if everyone were to hide away their money instead of spending it, the economy would get even worse. Businesses would make less money and would need to lay off more workers. Those people who thought they were being clever by saving their money may soon find themselves out of a job as a result! This strange reality is known as the "paradox of thrift". (A paradox is an idea that logically seems incorrect, but is in fact correct.)

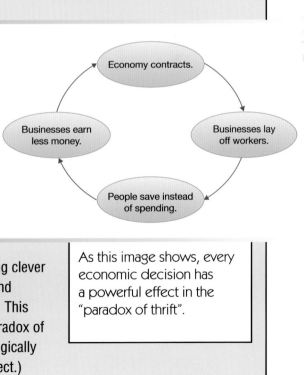

As this image shows, every economic decision has a powerful effect in the "paradox of thrift".

Government debt

You might wonder why governments don't just keep cutting taxes and increasing spending until the economy is growing. They don't do so because these measures decrease the money governments have available. If governments are spending more than they are taking in, they go into debt.

Central banks and lowered interest rates

Governments are not the only institutions that can help pull a country out of a recession. A central bank can play a hand by taking steps that encourage people to spend their money instead of saving it.

During the recent recession, many car dealers tried to attract buyers by offering low interest rates, good trade-in prices, and huge discounts.

Cutting rates to help end the recession

During the recent global financial crisis, central banks tried to lessen the effects of the economic downturn by lowering interest rates. In 2009 the Bank of England reduced the interest rate to 0.5 percent, the lowest rate in the 300-year history of the bank! Other countries also lowered interest rates to spur spending and investments.

In the United States, by the end of 2008, the Federal Reserve (the central bank of the United States) had dropped the interest rate to 1 percent. In late 2008 it was lowered even more, to between 0 and 0.25 percent! This meant that a US$1,000 loan only cost US$2.50 in annual interest in 2009. In 2007 it would have cost US$52.50.

As we have seen, a central bank can encourage people to spend by affecting interest rates (see box on page 30). By lowering interest rates, banks encourage people and businesses to borrow money. A lower interest rate also makes it easier for banks to borrow, which encourages them to lend more money.

Remember that borrowers and lenders make up the credit market. Lower interest rates speed up the flow of money from banks to borrowers to businesses, whose increased sales are signs of improvement in the economy.

Spending beyond one's means

While low interest rates can have positive effects on an economy, they can also cause problems. They encourage people to live beyond their means. Sometime people borrow money without having plans of how to pay back the money. This leads to people being unable to repay their debts.

During the first decade of the 2000s, low interest rates encouraged many people to use credit to pay for consumable items, meaning items that are only used once, such as going out to eat or taking a holiday. Many people could not pay back the money. This led to huge amounts of credit card debt and loan **defaults** (failure to pay a debt), because people had spent well beyond what they could pay back. Financial planners recommend not building up credit card debt on these kinds of purchases.

Taking too many risks

Low interest rates can also encourage banks to make riskier loans. As we have seen, when central banks lower interest rates, they also increase the money supply. If banks have more money to use for loans, then they will make more loans. After all, this is how they make money. Often, though, lots of available money also encourages banks to make loans that they would not otherwise make – loans that have lower chances of being repaid (see pages 42 and 43).

Depressions

There is an old joke that says, "A recession is when your neighbour loses his or her job. A depression is when you lose your job". That is not quite true – but what is a depression?

Depressions are large downturns in a country's economy. They present the same problems as recessions, but these problems are more severe. And during a depression, all of these economic hardships last even longer than in a recession.

The GDP drops significantly – by 10 percent or more. Unemployment is unusually high. With many people out of work, consumers spend even less money on goods and services. This decrease in sales forces businesses to cut their overall production.

Less production means companies need even fewer workers, and the unemployment rate continues to rise. Because businesses are doing poorly and confidence in the economy is low, share prices drop. Soon the values of major shares drop, and the stock market crashes.

After 2007, many highly skilled workers, like these, were out of work. As the downturn continued and more people lost their jobs, many feared another depression was about to begin. Fortunately, the recession never turned into a depression this time.

Many companies file for bankruptcy, because they cannot make enough money to pay their bills. When companies close, more people lose their jobs. This leads to less consumption, falling GDP, and even lower consumer confidence. Soon being able to afford even basic needs becomes difficult.

Japan's lost decade

Since World War II, most industrialized countries have suffered only recessions, not depressions. The one exception may be Japan. From 1989 to 1998, Japan suffered what some people call a "lost decade". Some business analysts argue that Japan's 10-year economic downturn was close to a depression, even though GDP did not drop 10 percent.

In the 1980s, Japan had an economic boom fuelled by low interest rates and overvalued **assets** such as housing and stocks. Low interest rates set by Japan's central bank, the Bank of Japan, meant that more money was available to lend and that borrowing was less expensive. This encouraged both banks and individuals to borrow even more money, which can eventually lead to risky investments.

Then in 1989, the Bank of Japan raised interest rates, which made borrowing more expensive and decreased the amount of money in the economy for lending. It also led to a sharp drop in the prices of overvalued assets. There was a 60 percent drop in the Japanese stock market, followed by a 70 percent drop in the value of properties from 1990 to 1994.

Banks that held property investments lost a lot of money. Many people defaulted on their loans. The losses and defaults left banks with less money to lend, and people and businesses with less money to borrow.

Both consumption and investment fell, as people and businesses spent less. In 1997 the Japanese government raised the tax on items used for consumption by 2 percent. Consumption fell even more, and the economy spiralled downward.

During this period, Japan's economy was stagnant, or not growing. In the 1980s, the Japanese economy averaged 4 percent annual growth. But in the 1990s, this growth shrunk to 1 percent a year. This economic downturn lasted 10 years, with sharp decreases in consumer spending, product sales, business investments, and share prices.

The Great Depression

As we have seen, in the 1920s the economies of the United States and many other countries were growing (see page 20). Companies earned more profits and grew. Those people investing in businesses earned more money and enjoyed higher standards of living. (However, it should be noted that average workers and farmers did not see much change in their standards of living.)

But when the good life ended, it crashed. The worldwide depression that followed devastated economies around the world. Here is what happened.

United States: In October 1929, the US stock market crashed, and millions of people lost their money. Eventually people bought fewer goods and services. Companies cut production and fired workers. Unemployment rose and banks failed, as people were unable to repay loans. By 1933 the GDP fell by about 30 percent. Unemployment rose to 25 percent in 1933, and was still 15 percent by the end of the decade.

Canada: Canada's businesses began failing. In 1929 Canadian companies earned US$396 million in profits. But by 1933, they had losses of US$98 million. In that same year, unemployment hit 27 percent, which meant that almost three million Canadians were out of work. Consumer spending slowed, and exports were cut in half. Between 1929 and 1933, Canada's GDP fell by 43 percent.

United Kingdom: The UK economy entered a severe depression at the start of 1930, with steep drops in the number of goods and services produced. Some areas were hit harder than others. For example, in Glasgow, 30 percent of the people were out of work, while in Newcastle, 70 percent of people were unemployed.

Germany: Germany was perhaps the hardest-hit European nation. After suffering hyperinflation in 1923, Germany was trying to revive its economy. But with the Great Depression, it was dealt another economic blow. Many historians believe that Germany's desperate economic situation made it possible for Adolf Hitler to rise to power during the 1930s.

Other areas: Some countries in Latin America suffered from economic depressions in 1929 or 1930. Japan also entered a depression in 1930, but its economic downturn was less severe than the depressions in the United States, Canada, and Europe.

Bank failures

During these depressions, people had trouble paying back money that they borrowed from banks. Afraid of losing more money, banks slowed their lending. Banks also had less money to make new loans. In need of cash, banks asked their borrowers to repay their existing loans. But people could not repay them, and banks failed.

When banks closed, their depositors lost their money. Then people had less (if any) money to spend, even on basic needs like food. Help did not come for unemployed workers, failing banks, or their depositors. Many people and companies could not even get loans to help them through the tough times.

People also feared that their banks would close and that they would lose their money. They had lost confidence in the banking system. So, they rushed to withdraw their money. These actions are called bank runs. Because banks lend out most of the money they take in, they were unable to repay all the people who demanded their money back.

WHAT IT MEANS TO ME   ## Depositor's insurance

Today, many countries have some kind of depositor's insurance. This insurance protects people who keep their money in banks. So, even if a bank fails, people do not lose all of their money. People can feel safe keeping their money in the bank. And banks can be confident that they will have this money to make loans and to earn more money.

Most banks and building societies have this insurance. If you decide to open an account, make sure that your bank is insured. That way you will know that your money is protected, even if the bank fails. You can also find out the maximum amount of money that is protected. For example, in the United Kingdom, each account is protected up to a maximum of £50,000.

Depositor's insurance has put an end to most "bank runs", like this one.

The credit cycle

A huge part of the economic cycle is the flow of credit, meaning money that is borrowed.

Fast forward into your future. You want to buy a new car, but you do not have the money. "No problem", you think. "I'll just borrow it". You head down to the bank or building society and apply for a loan. Thanks to credit, you will be driving away in a new set of wheels.

The credit market

The credit market is made up of borrowers and lenders. People, banks, and governments can be both borrowers and lenders by using and offering credit. To buy a car, you were the borrower and the bank was the lender.

But how does someone else putting money in the bank help you get a car loan? And how does the bank make money when you borrow money to buy a car? These are all parts of the credit cycle. The credit cycle has three basic parts:

1. People make **deposits**.

2. Banks and building societies give loans.

3. Businesses make products.

Making deposits

Banks are where the credit cycle begins. In order to function and to begin the credit cycle, banks need to take in money as deposits – for example, when you put money into a savings account. Banks pay you interest for keeping some kinds of accounts with them.

Many people depend on loans from banks, in the form of credit cards, to make big purchases.

Giving loans

The bank then uses this deposited money to begin the next step of the credit cycle: to make loans, such as your car loan, or to issue credit cards.

Banks make money by charging interest on the loans they give to borrowers. Banks charge higher interest rates on their loans than they pay to their customers. That is how a bank makes money. The more loans that a bank makes, the more money it can earn.

Banks not only lend money – they borrow it, too. Banks borrow money from each other and the central bank. They borrow to have enough money in safekeeping and to make more loans. When a bank borrows money, it has to pay interest.

The power of interest

Interest keeps the credit cycle going. People earn money from the interest payments that they receive from banks, and their bank balances grow. Banks earn money from the interest payments that they receive from their loans. They make more loans by using both the money that they earn from loans and the increased bank balances. And the cycle begins again.

Making products

Once money has been borrowed, people and businesses spend it. Businesses borrow money to pay for expenses, like building more factories and equipment. Businesses can also raise money by issuing shares and bonds (see box below). Regardless of how they get their money, this money allows businesses to grow. This, in turn, leads to the last step of the cycle: the businesses create products to sell.

Making money from shares and bonds

In addition to getting money from loans, some businesses also raise money by issuing shares and bonds. If a company issues shares, it pays dividends only if the company makes a profit. The more profit it makes, the more in dividends the owners of the shares will expect. But if the company makes no money or loses money, it does not have to pay dividends. In contrast, if a company issues bonds, it must pay the people who bought the bonds a fixed amount of interest, no matter whether the company makes a profit or loses money.

As we have seen, when businesses are successful and the economy is healthy, people and businesses have more money to spend and invest. Using this money, they can begin the cycle again, by putting their money in banks.

How the credit cycle flows

As we have seen, there are clear steps in the credit cycle: people make deposits, banks give loans, and businesses make products. But the flow of the credit cycle is what makes it all possible. When credit is flowing smoothly, the money can be exchanged and economies can expand. This diagram shows how it should happen:

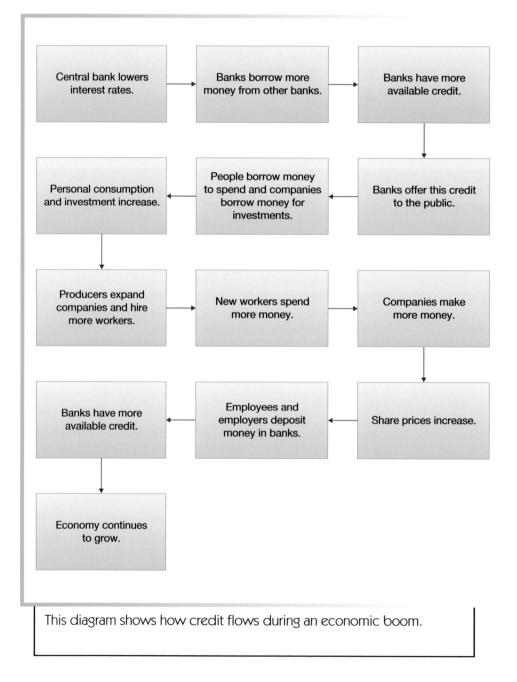

This diagram shows how credit flows during an economic boom.

But sometimes credit does not flow freely. Just as free-flowing credit can fuel economic growth, tight credit can slow down an economy. This diagam shows how this happens:

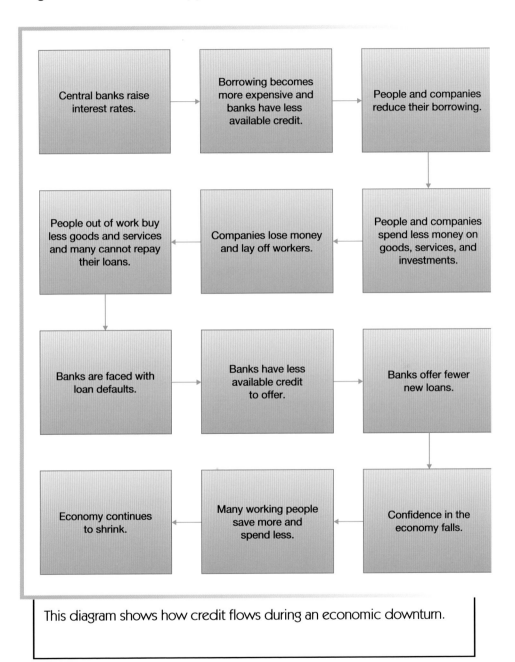

Central banks raise interest rates.

Borrowing becomes more expensive and banks have less available credit.

People and companies reduce their borrowing.

People out of work buy less goods and services and many cannot repay their loans.

Companies lose money and lay off workers.

People and companies spend less money on goods, services, and investments.

Banks are faced with loan defaults.

Banks have less available credit to offer.

Banks offer fewer new loans.

Economy continues to shrink.

Many working people save more and spend less.

Confidence in the economy falls.

This diagram shows how credit flows during an economic downturn.

Booms and crises

Sometimes, when credit is flowing, people become overly eager to find money-making investments. Instead of saving their money, they look for ways to invest it. They may not look for the wisest or safest investments.

Speculative bubbles

Sometimes people look for the hot investment that everyone is talking about – even if the price becomes sky high. In situations like these, a speculative **bubble** can form. **Speculation** occurs when people think, but do not know, that the value of the items will continue to rise. A bubble is any market in which the price of an item has gone far above what its normal market value would be. In speculative bubbles, items become overpriced due to speculation.

What causes bubbles?

No two bubbles are the same, but many share some of the same qualities. First, easy credit makes it profitable for people to invest in an asset, even at a high price. Often the asset becomes known as a good investment, and people come to believe that it is somehow different from other investments. The excitement around the asset makes people willing to pay more for it than they normally would. When people buy the asset in the hopes of reselling it at a higher price, it drives up the asset's price even higher.

The flower bubble

In the 1630s, people in the Netherlands developed "tulip mania". It all started when Conrad Gesner imported the first tulip bulb from present-day Turkey. Soon many people wanted to own tulips. The value of the flower's bulbs increased. People traded tulip bulbs in the same way they trade shares today. At one point, the price of the tulip bulb increased to 20 times its original value in one month. So, if you bought a tulip bulb for £100, it would have been worth £2,000 a month later. During the tulip bubble, a tulip bulb could sell for £50,000!

Speculative "bubbles" have developed for a variety of products, including tulips.

Eventually, the bubble "bursts". The price of the overvalued asset drops, and people who are left holding the asset suffer big financial losses – so big that the losses often lead to economic downturns.

Bubbles throughout history

Bubbles have occurred throughout history. People spent huge amounts of money on tulip bulbs in the Netherlands in the 1630s, only to have the bubble burst (see box on page 40). A bubble in Japanese shares and property prices contributed to the country's 10-year downturn in the 1990s (see page 33). Internet shares rose to great heights before crashing in 2000 (see box below). And between 2000 and 2006, housing prices rose unrealistically high in the United States, United Kingdom, and other countries, before the bubble burst – resulting in a global recession, as we will see in the next chapter. By 2010 these countries were slowly recovering from a global recession, but the path back to expansion remained uncertain (see page 49).

The dot-com bubble

From 1995 to 2000, a bubble in Internet shares formed. It was known as the "dot-com bubble", after the web addresses of the Internet-based companies. Many people invested in these new companies despite the companies' lack of profits. People believed that the companies' sales would soon take off as the Internet became more common. At one time, hundreds of new companies were being formed each week. Internet companies were overvalued, but demand was still rising.

Newspapers, magazines, and television news stories helped to fuel this bubble. They reported that dot-com companies would change the world, leading many people to justify the high price of their shares. The media also reported that people were making millions of dollars overnight by investing in dot-com companies. This also made people even more eager to buy these assets. Only later did investors realize that these assets were overvalued, and by then it was too late.

In January 2000, almost 20 Internet companies paid US$2 million each to advertise during the American football Super Bowl game. By this time, the value of technology shares had doubled in a year. But one year later, the value of the US stock market was cut in half as the dot-com bubble "burst". People around the world lost millions as the small Internet companies they had invested in went out of business, many without ever earning a profit.

The property bubble

In 2001 the world began an economic boom that was fuelled by free-flowing credit and an overvalued asset. The overvalued asset was property. Both the price and demand for homes continued rising for years. And people used these rising values to borrow more money, which was available at low interest rates.

House prices soar

House prices in the United Kingdom and the United States soared during the housing boom. Beginning in 1996, UK house prices rose non-stop for over 10 years. From 2001 to 2006, the prices of homes in the United Kingdom increased by 90 percent.

In the USA in 2001, the average price of a house in California was US$262,000. By 2005 it was US$532,000 – more than double! During these years, the price of houses rose by 70 percent in 10 states and in the District of Columbia. Yet within this same time, the general price level of goods and services only rose by 13 percent. House prices were high and rising faster than inflation.

Many believed that they had to buy property immediately before the prices got even more outrageous. Others hoped to get rich quick, investing in property only to sell it again at a later date as prices rose still higher.

Low interest rates

During the housing boom, the central banks in many countries were offering low interest rates. As we have seen, low interest rates encourage people and companies to borrow money. In order to keep interest rates low, the central banks put more money into the economy. This meant that banks had more money to lend. Lots of cheap credit encouraged people and companies to borrow more money than they could pay back. At one point, US companies were borrowing US$40 for every US$1 they earned.

Property prices rose in the first decade of the 2000s, but loans were easy to get. So, people kept buying more expensive property.

Reselling loans
Usually a bank that offers a loan has a good reason to make sure the loan is repaid. If the borrower does not pay back the loan, the bank loses the money. But during the housing boom, loose regulations gave banks and other financial institutions a way around this. Banks began to sell the loans to other investors. If the borrowers did not pay back the loans, the investors would lose out, not the banks.

In the United States, government-sponsored **mortgage** lenders Fannie Mae (for the Federal National Mortgage Association) and Freddie Mac (for Federal Home Loan Mortgage Corporation) bought many of these mortgages from banks. They kept some of the mortgages and then also resold others to members of the public as an investment. They also created loose restrictions for who could receive their loans.

Subprime lending
Suddenly, a lot of people who could not afford to pay back their loans were nonetheless given them. These people, many who earned small salaries or had defaulted on loans before, are known as **subprime borrowers**. (Prime borrowers are people who are more likely to pay back their loans.)

Often these new borrowers did not understand their loan terms. Many people agreed to loans that would not require a high payment at first, but would increase dramatically after a few years. More and more people were also allowed to take out loans without making a large deposit, which is an initial payment that is common with mortgages (property loans). With so many more people qualifying for loans and creating a demand for homes, the prices of houses rose even higher. But when many of these people could not repay their mortgages, those prices were sure to come down.

Profiting from the housing bubble
Many people profited from the housing bubble. Investors bought property and then resold for huge profits when the values increased. Individuals bought houses and then used their rising home values to borrow more money to spend. Large investment firms made money by grouping many home mortgages together in packages. The packages were then divided into pieces that were sold to smaller-scale investors.

There were economic booms around the world fuelled by the property bubble and cheap credit. Economies in the United States, Canada, Europe, Japan, and China were growing. People were buying more goods and services, both at home and from other countries. Companies were expanding both at home and in other countries. Unemployment was falling, and people were enjoying higher standards of living.

The global financial crisis

An economic boom fuelled by a bubble and cheap credit will not last forever. Eventually, people stop paying prices based on future values, and the price of the overvalued asset will fall. Central banks will eventually raise interest rates, because there are costs to keeping interest rates low, such as inflation (see pages 12 to 14).

The beginning of the end

When the price of houses came down, the economies of many industrialized nations, including the United Kingdom and the United States, suffered, too. In 2007, the BBC reported that the "credit crisis" had begun when US and European banks lost billions.

This all started, in part, when loose regulations allowed banks to issue mortgages to people who, as we have seen (see page 43), did not have the ability to make the monthly payments. This was very risky, but the banks were doing whatever they could to make a profit. It did not take long for many of these homeowners to realize they were too deeply in debt. Many of them tried to resell their homes, but they could not find buyers because the houses were overpriced.

When the borrowers began to default on their mortgages, banks, other financial institutions, and the people who bought the mortgages from the original lenders as an investment, began to lose money. Some banks and other financial institutions began to fall apart. Because people defaulted on their loans, banks were left with less money to lend.

Worldwide recession

When the property bubble burst, it was a disaster. Economies suffered downturns worse than anything since the Great Depression of the late 1920s and early 1930s. The collapse of the housing market spread across the economy. Financial institutions lost large amounts of money, were left with assets worth less than their original price (called "toxic assets"), and struggled to survive. Companies in North America, Europe, Asia, and Latin America were failing. Millions of people lost their jobs.

Once again, economic booms fuelled by cheap credit and overvalued assets ended in recessions around the globe.

Lehman Brothers and Bear Stearns

During the housing boom, US investment banks like Lehman Brothers and Bear Stearns made millions of dollars by creating and selling **funds** that contained only subprime mortgages. At that time, Bear Stearns was the fifth-largest investment bank in the United States, and Lehman Brothers was a global financial firm.

When the price of property dropped and more borrowers began to default on their loans, these companies lost billions of dollars. They were unable to pay their bills and were in danger of closing. Lehman and Bear Stearns had offices around the world. If these firms closed, then they would take millions of jobs and people's savings with them.

Both companies did end up failing. The US government convinced a US bank, JP Morgan Chase, to buy Bear Stearns before it completely went under. But JP Morgan Chase knew Bear Stearns was holding many overpriced mortgages, so the bank would not pay much. During the property boom, a share in Bear Stearns sold for US$160 per share, but JP Morgan paid US$2 a share. So, if you owned 100 shares in Bear Stearns, you would have had US$16,000 in shares during the housing boom. But when the company was sold, they were worth just US$200.

This kind of loss was happening to people around the world, including those with investments in Lehman Brothers. When this international firm went bankrupt, people lost their life savings – money that was going to be used to pay for education, retirement, and other long-term goals.

Many people also lost their jobs. Although Lehman was headquartered in New York City, the company had large offices in other countries. For example, about 4,000 people in the United Kingdom lost their jobs when Lehman's London office closed. In Japan, Lehman's closing increased the number of homeless people. Lehman Brothers was eventually bought by Barclays Bank, based in the United Kingdom.

Millions of people lost their jobs when the property market crashed. People like this Lehman Brothers employee packed their office belongings in boxes and permanently left their jobs.

The crisis continues

The property boom of the 2000s ended in a housing **bust**. And the credit expansion fuelled by a bubble and low interest rates ended in a deep recession. As investment firms and other companies failed, people lost their jobs and their savings. They also lost confidence in the economy. Many people said the world was headed for another depression.

Around the world, governments and central banks worked to restore confidence in their economies. They hoped that banks would begin to lend money again, people would begin to spend again, and companies would begin to grow again.

Credit crunch

Banks around the world had traded the subprime mortgages that were now going bad. Now nobody knew how many bad loans each bank had, and which banks might go bankrupt as a result. Banks were afraid to lend to each other, and money stopped flowing. Businesses could not get the loans they needed to keep their businesses growing, and people could not get the loans they needed to buy things. This lack of credit is known as a credit crunch.

Credit crunches make it harder for economies to come out of downturns. Economic growth mainly comes from consumer spending. And business investments make more jobs and also keep the economy growing. But when there is a credit crunch, there is less money available to borrow for consumption and investment. This makes the downturn even longer and more severe.

Iceland goes bankrupt

Iceland was one of the countries hurt most during the worldwide recession. Banks in Iceland had gone deeply into debt to expand and have an international role during the first decade of the 2000s. But when other banks stopped lending, Icelandic banks were unable to find a way to pay for their debt. As a result, in 2008 Iceland, as a whole country, went bankrupt.

Just like companies that needed bailouts to keep going, Iceland also asked for a bailout from the International Monetary Fund (IMF). The IMF is an international organization. The IMF gave Iceland a loan of several billion dollars to help the country survive this hard time.

Central banks step in

During the housing boom, interest rates were low. But central banks lowered them even more. In fact, as we have seen, the United States lowered its rates to almost zero, and the UK dropped its rates to the lowest levels in 50 years. Central banks hoped that by lowering interest rates and by making more money available for lending, banks would offer more credit. Then, people and businesses would start spending again, and the economy would grow.

Governments step in

Governments also tried to help banks during this economic downturn. The loan defaults had led to large losses for the banks. Governments tried to rescue big banks that were failing. In the United Kingdom, two big banks, Royal Bank of Scotland (RBS) and Halifax Bank of Scotland (HBOS), almost collapsed until the government provided massive financial support to the banking industry.

In 2005 and 2006 the United States did not have any bank failures. But by the end of 2009, more than 140 US banks had failed.

The US government also provided money to banks such as Bank of America, Citigroup, and other large companies to keep them in business. The large international Insurance company American International Group (AIG), which had provided insurance for bad loans, was given more than US$100 billion in government funds. The government also took control of car makers General Motors and Chrysler, which were near collapse due to the economic downturn.

Many governments worldwide believed that these businesses were "too big to fail", because letting them fail would cause an even worse economic downturn. But since there was not enough tax revenue to cover the **bailouts**, the government debt in the UK and the USA vastly increased. Economists tried to figure out the best path forward (see page 49).

During the recent recession, US car makers like GM (which owns GMC trucks, shown here) were hit especially hard. This had an impact on their European companies, too.

To sum it up

Cycles are patterns. They repeat themselves. The economic cycle is a repeating pattern of economic growths and downturns.

Living in booms and recessions

Since the 1990s, many countries in the world have seen both an economic boom and a recession. They have also seen bubbles, including the property bubble. In the early 2000s, as the prices of property continued to rise, people spent more money, businesses made more money, and industrialized countries around the world entered a time of growth in total output.

Then, at the end of 2007, many economic indicators peaked, and what followed were some of the worst economic downturns in modern history. As the economy sank, many people lost their jobs, their homes, and their savings. Assets that were once valuable lost their worth, and the world economy started to fall apart. People continued to spend less money, which made the recession even worse. Economic booms fuelled by the property bubble and cheap credit were over.

Looking forward

Countries rushed to save their economies. Governments spent more money and took over banks and companies. Central banks lowered the cost of borrowing money and put more money in the economy. And everyone hoped that these actions would push their economies past the downturn and into another boom.

Indicators of economic growth

Economic indicators show you where the economy is within the economic cycle. The following economic indicators can be noted when the economy is growing, and money is flowing through the economy:

- The GDP is growing.
- Companies are making more goods and services.
- People are spending more money.
- Businesses are growing, and new businesses are opening.
- Investors are making money from rising prices of assets and/or rising share prices.
- Businesses are hiring more workers.
- People are often borrowing more money to spend.

Indicators of an economic downturn

An economic downturn means that the economy is growing slower. The following economic indicators can be noted during an economic downturn, when money is flowing out of the economy:

- The GDP is falling.
- Companies are making fewer goods and services.
- People are spending less money.
- Businesses are cutting costs or closing.
- Investors are losing money from falling investment prices.
- Businesses are sacking workers and not hiring new workers.
- There is often not a lot of money for people to borrow.
- Many people and businesses get into greater debt because they are unable to pay their bills.

The flow of money

Money that flows through the economy also tells us about the economic cycle.

So, where are we now?

In early 2010 the economies of the United Kingdom, the United States, and most of Europe were recovering slowly from the recession. As usually happens early in a recovery, unemployment rates remained very high.

During such recovery periods, companies are usually afraid to hire new people right away, because they are not certain the recovery will be strong enough to get them new customers. Once consumers start to spend more, companies are usually willing to hire new people, which helps turn a recovery into an expansion. Unemployment usually begins to fall after that. Economists had different predictions for when this would be the case with the recent recession.

In early 2010 the central banks in the United Kingdom, the United States, and Europe kept interest rates low to make sure that businesses and households could borrow money at low rates. They did not want to raise rates too soon, because they were afraid that they might push the economy back into recession.

During this period the property market was still having trouble, mainly because unemployment was still very high. Most governments in the United Kingdom, the United States, and Europe were trying to make sure the recovery continued. Governments were still spending more money than usual to make up for the reduced spending by companies – all in the hope that another period of expansion would soon begin.

Timeline of the 2007–2010 economic crisis

2005	In some parts of the United States, house prices are more than double what they recently were.
2006	Within five years, the prices of homes in Spain have doubled, prices in the United Kingdom have risen by 90 percent, and prices in Ireland have risen by 71 percent.
2007 **June**	The US stock market index, the Dow Jones Industrial Average, drops almost 200 points. The Dow Jones includes 30 of the United States' largest companies. It reflects the average price of these companies' shares throughout the business day. Such a big drop among major companies signals problems for the economy. Two Bear Stearns investment funds, which contain subprime mortgages, go bankrupt.
July–August	Repossessions are on the rise, which means that banks are taking over properties that people cannot pay for. Soon California will have 2,000 new repossessions a day.
September	A crisis hits Northern Rock, a UK bank with many mortgage loans.
November	General Motors, a US car company, suffers one of the biggest quarterly (three-month) losses in US history.
December	Share prices plummet around the world.
2008 **June**	Property sales in the United Kingdom hit a 30-year low, and prices continue to drop.
September	US investment bank Lehman Brothers collapses. The US stock market suffers the biggest single-day drop in history, with the Dow Jones Industrial Average falling 778 points.

	Russia's largest stock exchange suffers its biggest one-day drop in 10 years.
	Stock markets in the United Kingdom, Germany, France, and Latin America crash.
	Japan suffers the largest drop in stock market history.
October	The country of Iceland goes bankrupt.
December	The International Monetary Fund predicts that most advanced countries, including the United States, United Kingdom, and Japan, will still be in a recession through 2009.
	In the United Kingdom, the Bank of England and the Treasury give banks £850 billion to keep the UK banking system going.
2009 **March**	The US government takes control of car companies General Motors and Chrysler as they spiral into bankruptcy.
June	US car company General Motors goes bankrupt.
November	According to the World Bank, 43 poor countries are still suffering from the global recession. These countries need US$11.6 billion more just to meet basic needs, including health care and education.
	The US bank holding company CITI Group files for bankruptcy.
	The unemployment rate in the United States tops 10 percent for the first time in 27 years.
December	The UK government owns about half of the Royal Bank of Scotland and Lloyds Banking Group.
2010 **January**	A GDP report shows that the US economy grew in the last six months of 2009, signalling that the recession possibly ended in the summer of 2009.
February	The country of Greece faces a possible default on its government bonds, hurting the confidence and economic prospects of European Union countries.

Glossary

annual yearly

asset valuable item

bailout loan or gift given to a company that is in danger of closing

bankruptcy when a court finds that a company is unable to pay its debts

bond investment that is a loan to the organization that sold it to you (usually a company or government) that pays a specified interest rate until a stated date

boom when an economy is growing unusually quickly, above trend

bubble when the price of an asset rises above what normal supply and demand conditions can explain

bust financial collapse

central bank country's main bank, with responsibilities that include issuing currency and regulating the credit supply

consumer buyer

consumer confidence when buyers believe that the economy is going to continue growing

consumption buying goods and services

contraction shrinkage

credit borrowing money to pay for a good or service

credit market where borrowers and lenders come together to receive and offer credit

currency money

cycle repeating pattern

debt money owed

default failure to pay back a loan or other debt

deflation when the general price level of goods and services drops and remains low

demand quantity of a good that consumers are willing and able to buy

deposit put money into the bank; also used to describe the money itself

depression very severe recession

dividend part of a profit that companies pay directly to shareholders (people who own shares in the company)

downturn when an economy's growth slows down

durable goods bought items that last for three years or more, such as cars

economic cycle time from one peak to another peak, including both an economic boom and a downturn

economic indicator measurements that describe economic activity, such as output, prices, and unemployment

economist person who studies how goods and services are made, bought, and distributed

economy system in which people make, sell, and buy goods and services

expansion growth

expense amount paid when buying a good or service

export good or service sold to another country; also used to describe the act of shipping off the product

fund managed sum of money intended for a certain purpose, such as earning more money from an investment

global worldwide

good item that can be bought and sold

Gross Domestic Product (GDP) total value of output produced in a country

Gross Domestic Product (GDP) per capita total value of output produced in a country divided by the population (number of people)

hyperinflation tremendous increase in the inflation rate, usually 100 percent or more

import good or service bought from another country; also used to describe the act of shipping in the product

income money earned

industrialized highly developed, in terms of business and manufacturing

inflation rise in the general price level of goods and services

interest cost of borrowing money; also, the rate of return for lenders

interest rate amount of money paid or received over the course of a year, as a percentage of the amount borrowed or loaned

invest put money into a financial product (such as shares or bonds) in hopes of earning more money

investment money that has been put into something, with the hope of making more money

loan agreement to lend someone money, with the understanding that the money will be repaid in the future, with interest

mortgage property loan, such as a loan to buy a house

peak highest point of the growth phase in an economic cycle

profit revenue minus costs

quantitative easing method by which a government or central bank increases the amount of money flowing into the economy by providing new money for the financial system. It is sometimes referred to as "printing money", but mostly it is electronic transfers of new credit.

recession fall in economic activity

revenue amount of money received when goods and services are sold

risk chance that something will turn out differently than expected

salary money earned from working; also called wages

service performed action

speculation financial risk taken with the hope of gain

standard of living comfort level from having goods, services, and luxury items available to you

share unit of ownership in a company, also called a stock

stock market place where buyers and sellers of shares and other securities come together

subprime borrower person who borrows money, but does not have a good chance of paying it back

supply quantity of a good or service that a business produces

tax fee that the government charges on items such as income and property

trade deficit when a country imports more goods than it exports

trade surplus when a country exports more goods than it imports

trend growth rate average growth rate for an economy in the long run

trough lowest point of an economic downturn

unemployment insurance benefits given to people who are not working and meet certain requirements

unemployment rate percentage of working-age people who do not have jobs

value benefit received from a good or service. Money is a common measure of value (as reflected in prices), although not all value can easily be measured in terms of money.

wages money earned from working; also called a salary

Find out more

Books to read

History in Literature: The Story Behind John Steinbeck's Of Mice and Men (Great Depression), Sharon Ankrum (Heinemann Library, 2006)

Life Skills: Managing Money, Barbara Hollander (Heinemann Library, 2009)

Life Skills: Raising Money, Barbara Hollander (Heinemann Library, 2009)

Political and Economic Systems: Capitalism, David Downing (Heinemann Library, 2008)

Show Me the Money, Alvin Hall (Dorling Kindersley, 2008)

Websites

www.bankofengland.co.uk/education
This is the education partition of the official website of the Bank of England.

www.banksafeonline.co.uk
This website is the UK banking industry organization that gives you advice about banking online and how to keep your money safe.

Index